IN THIS UNUSUAL AND
DELIGHTFUL BOOK ABOUT THE
WORLD'S MOST POPULAR
CARTOON CHARACTERS,

AUTHOR JEFFREY LORIA
REVEALS SOME FASCINATING
INSIGHTS INTO THE WHOLE
PEANUTS MYSTIQUE, AND SHOWS
WHY IT HAS CAUGHT AND HELD
THE IMAGINATION OF
READERS OF ALL AGES

ABOUT THE AUTHOR

JEFFREY H. LORIA is a man of many interests, from his fascination with the Peanuts kids to his life as art expert, teacher, and businessman. Long intrigued by the poignant philosophies of Charlie Brown and his friends, like millions of others throughout the world, Mr. Loria has followed the adventures of Charles Schulz' characters from the time he graduated from Yale University. Now completing his MBA at Columbia University, Mr. Loria teaches Art Connoisseurship at the New School for Social Research in New York City. Author of *Collecting Original Art,* now in its fifth printing, Mr. Loria soon hopes to introduce the Peanuts to the world of Fine Art through the medium of the original lithograph.

WHAT'S IT ALL ABOUT, CHARLIE BROWN?

PEANUTS KIDS LOOK AT AMERICA TODAY

BY JEFFREY H. LORIA

In collaboration with Pat K. Lynch

Contributing Editor: Susan Newman

A FAWCETT CREST BOOK

Fawcett Publications, Inc., Greenwich, Conn.

FOR VINCENT PRICE

THIS BOOK CONTAINS THE COMPLETE TEXT OF THE
ORIGINAL HARDCOVER EDITION.

A Fawcett Crest Book reprinted by arrangement with
Holt, Rinehart and Winston, Inc.

Library of Congress Catalog Card Number: 68-12212

Printed in the United States of America

CONTENTS

AUTHOR'S NOTE

●

I AM DEEPLY GRATEFUL TO THE ONE MAN WHO MADE this book possible—to Charles M. Schulz, for his genius, inspiration, and encouragement. I will never be able to thank him sufficiently for this opportunity.

I thank also James Hennessy and Harry Gilbert at the United Feature Syndicate, for having been so positive in their enthusiasm and cooperative in all areas.

To Susan Newman, my sincere thanks for her professional assistance in helping me to put this book together.

J.H.L.

1
.
WHAT'S
IT ALL ABOUT?

IF THERE WERE a Sigmund Freud award for valorous devotion to the art of living in a complex environment, the Peanuts would win it, hands down. Although they manifest an extraordinary number of neurotic symptoms, the Peanuts kids cope with them magnificently.

The kids are rarely overpowered by life's adversities, because they set up safety valves to release the mental anguish caused by their personal hang-ups. Lucy, for example, flaunts her femininity so she can cope with life more easily. Charlie Brown eats peanut butter sandwiches when he gets lonely. And Frieda wheedles compliments to restore her faith in herself and in her curly hair. Snoopy, unashamed, straps himself to his doghouse and mentally shrugs off most anything he can't handle.

All these defenses help the Peanuts to survive in an imperfect world. Each character has mastered in his own way the art of living in a society filled with pressures and problems. Linus has developed a unique philosophy called "Runism," which he employs when a personal problem arises.

Linus' philosophy is one used by a large segment of Americans today. And it is used widely whether people are running away from doing the dishes or from deciding on marriage or a new investment. Today's adult, faced with enormous business pressures and family problems, becomes a virtual expert at "Runism." Many feel that if you procrastinate long enough, the problem will evaporate. Unfortunately, this does not happen in our world or in the Peanuts' world either. And the Peanuts, unlike many members of our society, realize this to be true.

When situations get out of hand for the Peanuts, Lucy Van Pelt is always ready to provide private psychiatric consultation. For five cents, Lucy gives her expert advice.

14

It's a pity Lucy isn't available to the rest of the world. With her insight, and at that price, with a slight additional charge for slide projector and travel expenses, she would be a boon to the psychiatric profession. There are no stigmas attached to seeing this psychiatrist-in-residence. The Peanuts are very open about their five-cent consultations. They don't surreptitiously slip off at lunch for an hour "to do some shopping." In fact, Linus told Charlie Brown to his face that he thought Sally needed help.

Lucy gets most of her business from Charlie Brown. At first, she was hesitant about taking Charlie on because "by the time you're five, your character is well on the way to being established," she says. Charlie, like many five-year-olds today, has already developed an array of character fantasies—as well as some real problems. His lack of self-confidence, however, is well-founded. He loses all the baseball games he manages and the checker games he plays with Lucy. He can't ever fly his kite without getting it stuck in a tree. And his friends constantly make cutting remarks right to his face.

In one siege with his lady psychiatrist, Charlie ran up a phenomenal bill of $143.00. "And I still have the same faults!" remarked disgruntled Charlie when he heard the figure. Thousands of people invest millions of dollars and months of time to find themselves in the same predicament as Charlie when consultation is over. No noticeable change, no significant improvement.

There are many people like Charlie for whom psychiatry is not the answer. Because they don't know where they fit in, they are never really happy. They try one thing, then another. They may skip from town to town, job to job, mate to mate. They even try changing their personalities. They develop phony accents and resort to bacchanalian frolicking in an effort to avoid thinking about their situations. Others find solace in dependency on others. In a group, the vague feeling of uneasiness, manifested by many members of the Lost Generation, tends to alleviate itself.

In their quest for a philosophy to live by and a niche to live in, people often rely on the stars. They find a measure of security in charted horoscopes and daily astrological forecasts. Palmistry, tea leaves, numerology, and consultations with a favorite swami may envision the "pure pleasure" and sense of being loved that Snoopy experiences when he finds his favorite sherbet near his food dish.

Dabbling in hocus-pocus, making money, or being famous doesn't always provide security and happiness. Even Charlie Brown, who longs for a Valentine card or party invitation from one of his peers, knows that. History books are filled with stories of people who had a psychological need to be recognized. Some of them directed their energies toward the creative good. They contributed outstanding accomplishments in the arts, science, and government. Others, like Adolf Hitler and the German philosopher Nietzsche, directed such energies to misguided and destructive ends. "Their characters were established bad," Lucy might analyze.

17

What's the answer? How does one find happiness and security? The Peanuts would go along with Aristotle on that one—"Know thyself."

The Peanuts know themselves fairly well. Charlie, for example, explains that he's the kind of person people just naturally take advantage of. And Lucy, who hates to admit anything, displays a definite self-understanding.

Linus comprehends his psychological quirk. He is quite open about needing his blanket to face the harsh realities of life. And he is well aware that his blanket represents the inner security that he is lacking. He agrees with Lucy when she says that his blanket is his "spiritual tourniquet." He even *tries* to give it up. That's more than can be said for people who won't take a plane because they never did it before, or for people who can't sleep without a sleeping pill because they have been taking one every night for the past six years.

Snoopy has his own addictions. But like Linus, he is completely aware of them. At first Snoopy stood under a water sprinkler to cool himself off and brighten his outlook. Eventually this pleasant pastime turned into a terrible threat. "I've become a compulsive water sprinkler-head stander," he says. "Once I start something I always overdo it!"

Snoopy realizes how easy it is to become addicted to something pleasurable, like a water dish or ice cream. But Snoopy knows his needs are no different from those of an alcoholic, chain-smoker, drug addict, or compulsive eater. He needs some outside help to overcome his sprinkler temptation. Fortunately, Lucy turns the sprinkler off for him.

Snoopy, Linus—all the Peanuts need a little push from the outside to help them overcome their psychological barriers.

Frieda is the only Peanut who never admits that she has problems or needs help. A quick look under the surface, however, exposes Frieda's constant need for reassurance.

Frieda is like most of us—less prone to admit our hangups. She doesn't acknowledge who she is as straightforwardly as the rest of the kids. Even little Sally openly discusses her emotional makeup. She has "guilt feelings" because her brother must wheel her in the stroller during prime baseball time. She admits her fears and expresses her thoughts as only a very honest, frank person would do.

When such a feeling of futility crops up, the Peanuts are bright enough to seek professional assistance. Lucy is perhaps more honest and less tactful than a real psychiatrist dares to be.

Lucy, however, can be very helpful at times. She has a lot to say about inner childhood fears, frustration, inhibition, sublimation, and the unconscious. On the other hand her pragmatic assertions about survival in a hostile world are upsetting rather than soothing.

For most people, Lucy's insights carry with them more reality than they can stand. The important thing about the Peanuts' psychology is that they *do* face reality. They even pay five cents for the hard, cold "real" facts.

The Peanuts can cope with living in our society because they accept their personal limitations, while they continually search for more self-awareness and understanding. They're not able to delude themselves when asked, "What's it all about?"

2
.

GIVE ME
ONE REASON
TO LEAVE
HOME

JUST BECAUSE YOU'RE related to people doesn't mean
you have to like them!" Lucy advised Snoopy after he
found his family reunion disappointing. Other Americans seem to follow Lucy's candid advice. A sister doesn't
talk to her brother for fifteen years; a daughter moves
away to avoid the "tyranny" of her father; a father dis-
owns his son. These familial situations are all prevalent
in today's society.

When it comes to roots, the Peanuts resemble clannish
ethnic groups before they became Americanized and their
members became independent of each other. For the Peanuts, the home is the most stable unit they know! The
kids don't "find themselves" by moving away to live on
their own. They don't go bopping off to Nepal or Tangier
to find the real meaning of life. In fact, the idea of leav-
ing home for even a short time shakes their equilibrium.

The mere suggestion of a summer sojourn to camp is unsettling to the Peanuts. Even Lucy, probably the most independent one, reacts to such an idea.

Ten minutes on a camp bus is all it takes to make Charlie Brown feel lonesome. "I feel like I'm being drafted," he declares. And Linus finds separation from the family so disquieting that he suffers from fears of desertion. "What if Mother and Dad move away while I'm gone, and don't tell me?" he moans, lying disconsolately in his camp bunk.

The Peanuts are as attached to their friends and neighbors as they are to their mothers and fathers, sisters and brothers. The small folks have little in common with children from the big city, who seldom get to know their neighbors. These young sophisticates have accepted "coming and going" in a mobile society. A nod in an elevator or a demi-smile in the street is all the interaction the urban child expects.

Many contemporary school children look for any excuse to break away from home and neighborhood. They revel in camp, pajama parties, and boarding school. The Peanuts are a more dependent lot. They love and respect the ties that bind. Just look at Charlie Brown. He's not very fond of camp. He says he'll miss all his friends. Yet Charlie goes along year after year to please his parents.

The other Peanuts are just as respectful of their relatives. They may disagree with a particular wish, but they acquiesce to their elders. Linus, for instance, wages continual warfare with his grandmother every time she comes to visit. His grandmother uses brute force to get Linus' blanket away from him. Linus fights back with strategic plans, such as using a colored dish towel as a decoy. But, in the end, love and respect win out.

Few children today even take the time to talk with their grandparents. They are too busy applying body paint and reading about England's current singing rages.

Among the Peanuts, respect for family relationships becomes almost hero worship for Mom and Dad. Parents are held in high regard. There are no derogatory comments made behind their backs. The Peanuts stick up for parents. Charlie quickly goes to his father's defense when Violet gushes too effusively about her dad.

Probably the most noteworthy form of hero worship, and the biggest compliment that a parent can receive, is a child who wants to grow up just like his parent. Charlie Brown wants to be like his dad, with one minor alteration. Charlie would rather be a bus driver than a barber. And his sister, Sally, wants to be just like Mom.

Sally tells her mom that camp won't help either. "What good is camp if you plan to be a wife and mother?"

The "feminine mystique" is foreign to the Peanuts girls. As far as Sally and Violet are concerned, women are born to have homes and families. The need to prove themselves, to use female guile or masculine trickery in order to show that they can succeed in a man's world has not yet entered their minds. Much to Charlie's dismay, the girls comb their hair, discuss parties, and admire each other's clothes in the midst of a heated baseball game.

Only Lucy looks outside the home for complete fulfillment. She wants to work for an advertising agency when she grows up. In spite of her ambition, even Lucy doesn't ridicule the female role.

You never see a willfully disobedient Peanut, which is quite a contrast to the "spare-the-rod" school of children who kick parents or throw a temper tantrum when they don't get their own way. The Peanuts know the rules at home, and just how far they can waver before pushing the limits too far.

Many parents who raise their children permissively would say that such structured relationships might stunt the creative and emotional growth of a child. If asked, the Peanuts would not agree. The threat of no dinner or no television privileges is part of growing up. It doesn't hinder the Peanuts' close family ties.

Part of the explanation for the marvelous rapport between the Peanuts' generation and their parents' is the demonstrative tokens of love and affection the grown-ups give to their children. Peanut parents always find time to go to PTA meetings, Christmas pageants, Little League baseball games, and Schroeder's piano recitals. They instruct lovingly, and have confidence that their children will learn the right thing to do. The kids reflect this confidence.

38

Another explanation for the relatively untroubled relationship between the Peanuts and their parents is the kids' understanding of the grown-ups. They realize that parents have weaknesses and faults too.

Violet makes some wise observations about her father. She points out that within three days he had been to see a dentist, an ophthalmologist, and an orthopedist. And she notes that these visits to the doctor are "all part of his complete physical breakdown since turning forty."

Some of today's old-school parents would not permit their children to see their weaknesses, fearing a loss of respect. Such parents prefer to be perfection in their children's eyes, someone to emulate. Permissive contemporary parents, on the other hand, hold nothing from their children. They raise children with a candidness that a child cannot always comprehend.

The Peanuts' parents reveal their humanity with just the right dosage. They are human beings with weaknesses, as well as authority figures. Consequently, the Peanuts can identify with their parents, and at the same time can respect their authority. There is only one parental trait the Peanuts cannot understand.

The Peanuts like it at home. Their parents have a job to do. And just because they make demands now and then, and once in a while need a vacation—that's really no reason for the kids to run away from home.

3
·
THE
GOOD BOOK

JUST LIKE ALMOST everyone else in America today, the Peanuts are looking for a bit of solid ground to stand on. Some of us turn wholeheartedly to religion to increase our sense of security, belonging, and goodness. Others turn their backs on religion. Although the kids are religiously precocious, they are cautious about placing all their hope in the power of religion. The subjectivity of religious beliefs is quite clear to the little folks. The fact that people join religious and charitable organizations with not the best of motives would not shock the reality-oriented Peanuts clan.

Goodness and respectability do not come from religion alone—and the kids know it. You don't suddenly become virtuous because you attend Sunday School every week. Nor do you find the reasons for your existence by faithfully attending church—some leads, possibly. The Peanuts have their own less-than-formal religious theories about existence.

The kids avidly pursue what is morally good without preaching the tenets of organized religion. It is rare for them to be taken in by words and deeds brimming with conventional religious overtones. Yet their comments and actions reveal a sound understanding of the theological problems faced by mankind. For example, when Linus heard that Charlie Brown thought we were put on earth to make others happy, he said: "I guess I'd better start doing a better job. I'd hate to be shipped back!"

To the most earthbound, well-adjusted Peanut, Snoopy, the spiritual question of existence poses few problems and creates no boundless theological questions.

Charlie Brown, on the other hand, faces one perplexing problem after another. He finds what to do now that we are here a bigger barrier than the question of why we are here at all. From experience he knows that one must be meek not so much to "inherit the earth" but just to survive on it.

46

Linus, like most of us, often has grave problems coping with life. He, more than any other Peanut, relies on religion to explain the complex business of living. And Linus' theological conclusions are often reassuring, especially to worrywarts like Lucy.

But in day-to-day practical matters Linus forgets theological conjecture. His blanket and thumb provide all the security he needs. Once that monster dog Snoopy stole Linus' blanket. "I can't live without that blanket . . . I can't face life unarmed!" Linus whimpered. After the blanket-snatching incident Linus confided in Lucy. "If you can't trust dogs and little babies, whom can you trust?" he asked.

At times Linus, the loyal Church School student, thinks the answer to trust lies in religion. He turns to the Bible as a guide for living. But like most people, he finds something—be it fish every Friday, no transportation on Saturday, or church every Sunday—to prevent him from fanaticism.

The Peanuts are too young and trusting to have developed a rational skepticism about religion. Yet they do realize that in the course of today's trials and traumas many people hide behind religious façades in order to survive, protect themselves, or for self-interest. But for the kids, to become atheists, agnostics, or nihilists would be rash. They are still too preoccupied with what is good and evil, love and hate, to worry about whether or not they should believe in God.

This insight greatly disturbs Linus. He ponders the facts and complains to Charlie Brown of the constant fighting, quarreling, and battling going on in his soul. Finally, Linus tells Lucy he wants "to be all love!" Few people today take the time to consider what goes on within them. Even fewer attempt to do something about what they feel. But Linus follows Lucy's simple remedy. Just "lean a little to one side . . . see? Now the love will get a chance to spill over into the hate!" Lucy explains.

Charlie Brown also searches for ways to make his life more meaningful. And he does so without consciously cushioning his efforts with religious dogma.

Being products of Judaic-Christian culture, the Peanuts know all about sin and suffering. Even selfish Snoopy says, "Curse the Red Baron and his kind! Curse the wickedness in this world! Curse the evil that causes all this unhappiness!" Linus screams for "peace" within his quarreling heart. The doctrines relating to evil and suffering are deeply implanted in the kids. Occasionally Snoopy, like most contented beings, thumbs his snout at sin and retribution.

51

Charlie and Linus, however, take the business of sin quite seriously. Again, they have their own realistic rather than biblical interpretations of good and bad deeds. Linus finds suffering for the sins of others upsetting.

Charlie Brown, the world's biggest loser, has learned to live with such sorrow and disappointment. It's almost a way of life for him. Like many minorities throughout the centuries, Charlie bears the sins of the world on his shoulders. He accepts undeserved abuse just as certain religious and ethnic groups face persecution and blind prejudice.

The Peanuts *know* the correct and proper way to treat their fellow man. Sometimes, being human, they simply forget. They are searching for a good and righteous way to live. Their actions, as their words, however, prove they will be Good Samaritans just so long—no matter what the Good Book says.

4
.
I WILL NOT
TALK IN CLASS

EDUCATION IS SERIOUS business, especially for the Peanuts. The kids are real school-niks. Collectively they extol the virtues of the academic world. Even the little Peanut—Sally—after first balking at the idea of going to school, became an education aficionado.

But every now and then the kids express very typical anti-school attitudes. Charlie gets panicky about the prospect of twelve more years in school. Linus prefers watching television or staying in bed to attending classes with-

out his blanket. All the kids, at one time or another, rebel against academic authority. Generally, however, the Peanuts are pro-school and praise the advantage of being able to get an education.

Charlie and his pals certainly do not have much in common with today's high-school and college dropouts. For dropouts school is associated with conformity, the "Establishment." And they reject the "passport" into middle-class prosperity and mores that education offers. They would rather choose their own conformity—communal living in San Francisco's Haight-Ashbury or New York's East Village. They reject universal education for themselves to leave time to discuss universal love.

The Peanuts, on the other hand, neither reject nor rebel against society's educational standards. One vociferous Peanut, Linus, probably would never comprehend the dropout phenomenon.

59

Lucy, the most cynical of the group, is "a great believer in education." Someday she "intends to be the most educated person in the whole world . . . I'll never be satisfied until I'm too smart for my good!" she tells Charlie in her most serious tone. Like most kids Lucy sometimes gets sidetracked while heading toward her goal. Once, to her own mortification, she almost got expelled from nursery school. In true fussbudget form Lucy tackled her punishment.

On the whole, the Peanuts accept administration's rules and regulations. Lucy and Peppermint Patty choose inoffensive skirt lengths. The boys choose appropriate school attire and civilized hair lengths.

Even Charlie Brown, born rationalizer, does not bother to protest or analyze school. He knows the rules—obey and learn.

Calm acceptance of the administration is scarcely characteristic of contemporary students. As boys' tresses get longer, girls' dresses get shorter. Throwing eggs at the university president and marching in protest against early curfews are the "now" ways of dealing with school authorities. Of all the Peanuts, only Linus displays some ability and desire to upset the status quo.

Although Linus talks aggressively, he would never jeopardize the privilege of being able to go to school. All the Peanuts, including Snoopy, see the advantages that come from education.

The kids are cognizant of the concrete benefits presented by education for their future lives. "Knowledge for knowledge's sake" is not a dictum the Peanuts would uphold. Charlie knows that he can be a better bus driver after a sound basic course of general study. Lucy fully understands that she can get that job at an advertising agency only *after* she is properly educated. And Schroeder realizes that a concert pianist needs a well-rounded education in addition to his comprehensive studies of the piano.

A "good" education has other advantages. Achievement is held in high regard by teachers, parents, and peers. Failure is not "in" with these kids.

And that includes Mom and Dad. The kids have wise parents indeed! Although they are concerned with their children's progress, they avoid exerting too much pressure. Linus probably got the worst punishment for a bad report card. His father told him he couldn't play after school for a whole week. "What are you doing, studying?" Charlie Brown asked. "No, watching TV!" Linus calmly replied. There is a healthy give and take between Peanut parent and Peanut child in the realm of the academic.

Because there is so little shrieking and sobbing over report cards and class standing, the Peanuts exude enthusiasm for everything related to school—including teachers. As with their parents, the kids have warm, friendly relationships with their instructors. In fact, Linus dons rose-colored glasses when he talks about Miss Othmar.

But when it comes to downright interaction with Miss Othmar, Linus, like most intelligent children, changes his tune somewhat.

In the final analysis, however, Linus admits grudgingly that "the National Education Association is very lucky to have her [Miss Othmar]."

The Peanuts would not be the real kids they are if they didn't criticize the institution that occupies so much of their time. Charlie Brown makes a few cutting comments now and then. But Lucy has the most caustic indictment against American education.

68

These little students may get a bit negative at times, but fighting one teacher *who knows you* is better in their opinion than adjusting to an IBM card that punches out your grades. Or a "talking typewriter." Or a computer that tells you that you are last in the class of 700—with no explanation or discussion about it.

The kids are, for the most part, content in their "little red schoolhouse." The most they have to cope with is staying after school when they are bad—and "new math."

For contemporary students, however, the way one counts and how well does matter. If a student wants to get into the college of his choice—even his third choice—everything makes a difference, everything from the number of classmates he has and where he lives to the grades he gets and what he does with his free time. But these complex problems do not exist at the Peanuts' school. If you can use a handkerchief, get a drink of water, put on your own coat, and cut with scissors, you are in!

The Peanuts respect education rights. They try their very best and proudly display their hand-scrawled "A's." These small scholars are a world apart from the icy, impersonal class. Are there really students who are too busy protesting the ways of education to attend classes? they would ask. Even Sally would gaze quizzically at the student who cuts zoology class in order to march with a banner of protest in hand.

5

.

PASS
THE CRANBERRIES,
PLEASE

DOES YOUR SAYING 'Happy New Year' make it happy
. . . just because you say it, does that mean it will be?
—Is this a guarantee?" demands Lucy. All Charlie Brown
and his friends can do is try to make each year a happy
one. And they do try. They take advantage of every
holiday. They diligently observe the traditions and accept
the "fringe benefits" of each special day.

For them, Christmas isn't Christmas without real trees.
July 4th isn't Independence Day without loud firecrackers
and fancy-colored flares. And Easter isn't Easter without
chocolate bunnies and brightly dyed eggs. Holidays, birth-
days, and their own special celebrations fill their lives
with happiness and meaning, not with burdensome social
obligations to send presents or attend parties.

Beethoven's birthday is one special day Schroeder never
fails to celebrate. In fact, he goes the whole route for his
favorite composer: a cake, a card signed "from Schroeder

with love," and a rendition of "Happy Birthday" as only a pupil of Beethoven could play it. Schroeder even makes sure the other Peanuts know the exact day, just in case they want to join in the festivities.

Linus, just like many children, is not always content to celebrate days that belong to other people. "Mom has her day, Dad has his, why not children too?" Linus once asked. His grandmother promptly responded from the other room, "Every day is children's day."

Snoopy, too, considers ways to get his own special days. National Dog Week with its mealtime surprises, extra sleep, and above-par consideration is not enough for this very human dog.

While the kids may decide to celebrate John Doe's birthday or figure out some way to lengthen their holidays, they never fail to give all the usual legal and religious holidays the full treatment. Columbus Day, Election Day, Mother's Day—no important day passes them unnoticed.

On Valentine's Day—one of the most important to the kids—sincerity come first. In his gallant way Schroeder sums up the Peanuts' feelings about Valentine's Day: "I didn't want to give you the wrong impression. Sending a Valentine would have implied that I can stand the sight of you."

In the Peanuts' world you get a card only if you're high on the heart chart. Once Shermy discovered he had a secret love. Charlie Brown, however, discovered nothing new.

This honest approach would make some of our Valentine cards seem like hypocritical gestures—like the Valentine for the secretary who tells of your tardiness or one for the date who bores you but feeds you.

Even on Mother's Day the Peanuts kids simply can't be bothered with shallow pleasantries and gushy sentiment.

To the kids, serving mother breakfast in bed instead of playing baseball says much more than a bubble cape, mink or splashy diamond pin—even if they could afford it.

Dad gets his recognition and a flourish of appreciation too. Charlie and Lucy may not present Dad with a two year subscription to *Playboy* or a gold-engraved cigarette case, but they never fail to thank Dad on his day.

Unlike many of today's precocious children, the Pea
nuts know their place in the home. And they show they
know by the respect accorded Mom and Dad all year
'round as well as on their special calendar days.

There are certain traditions which must be respected on
a given day or within a given time period. They just
aren't as much fun at any other time. On February 22nd
doesn't every grammar-school girl want to play Martha
Washington in her husband's birthday pageant? And
after seeing the pageant, don't most little boys want to
chop down a cherry tree—any tree?

The Peanuts are no different. They put on skits and
recite poems about the first President. They eat cherry pie
and put great effort into interpreting the history of the
day.

Independence Day is one of the Peanuts' favorite historical events. The traditions of 1776 prevail for these arch patriots. Their spirit, however, doesn't seem to affect the adult world. For example, Manager Charlie Brown cancels all sports events in respect for the day. In all their patriotic fervor, it's no wonder they sometimes get confused.

79

Today's teeny-boppers and their older counterparts never get their holidays confused. They know months in advance—and to the minute—when each holiday will begin. And when that minute arrives, judging from the chaos at airports and train terminals, as many as can pile on the first planes and trains to Fort Lauderdale, Nassau, and Bermuda, and points south.

The Peanuts clan has never caught the Easter scene. They firmly believe that Easter, like Christmas, is a family together time—it's a holiday with serious meaning, not to be fooled with. Mom should get an Easter lily; Dad, a basket filled with goodies. And the kids—they'll settle for chocolate bunnies and jelly beans.

A milk chocolate bunny is certainly better than surviving on pot, LSD, and banana peels under palm trees to the tune of "Mellow Yellow." The little folks will gladly hunt for Easter eggs. Easter wasn't meant to be a ten-day excursion into the psychedelic.

It seems that some Easter "trip-takers" need marijuana and sugar cubes to loosen them up a for little fun or to activate their imaginations. Not the hearty Peanuts crew. A traditional holiday is enough to send them into a "tale-spin." The mere existence of Halloween inspired Linus Van Pelt to spin his fantastic Great Pumpkin story. If Linus were telling it now, he might tell this much: No one has ever seen "him." He rises out of the pumpkin patch, and flies through the air giving gifts to deserving boys and girls.

The Great Pumpkin bears a striking resemblance to Santa Claus. Linus, however, adamantly objects to any possible confusion. "Would I confuse the sun and the moon? Would I confuse NBC with CBS? Would I confuse the American League with the National League? Would I?" True believers—in anything—have a lot in common with Linus. They are sometimes subject to the mistaken visions of their own imaginative creations.

In spite of the fact that each of Linus' vigils has ended without a glimpse of the Great Pumpkin, his faith remains unshaken. His yearly watch is a ritual not to be forgotten.

81

Thanksgiving dinner is just one more tradition-filled event that Linus and his friends cannot overlook. No matter what Madison Avenue says is the "in" entree this Thanksgiving, you can be sure the Peanuts' plates will be piled high with turkey, dressing, and cranberry sauce. Only one Peanut is not permitted to join in the traditional celebration.

As Christmas approaches, the entire Peanuts clan fears they will be just like Snoopy at Thanksgiving—celebrating alone. Commercialism seems to be snatching away the true spirit of Christmas. And the kids are very concerned. They hold joint meetings to probe into the rumor that Santa Claus is controlled by some "big Eastern syndicate." After all, they have a right to be concerned.

Ol' Charlie is so distressed that he consults Psychiatrist Lucy to find out why he doesn't feel joyous about the coming Christmas season. Linus, on the other hand, knows precisely why his spirit is on the decline.

Even in his distraught state, Linus keeps up the Christmas spirit. That's more than can be said of Christmas shoppers in overcrowded stores.

The thinning spirit of Christmas begins to thicken everywhere as New Year's plans are set. With the beginning of a new year, the end of an old year, the Peanuts get reflective. Lucy says, "We need bigger years!" Would longer years be happier years for us?

Would years be more meaningful if everyone followed the Peanuts' rule—a holiday isn't a holiday unless it is celebrated the traditional, "let's-go-all-out" way? Or does it make any difference how you celebrate?

6

PEANUT BUTTER
OR
UNREQUITED LOVE

IN LOVE'S ARENA hope keeps the Peanuts hopping. For the small folks, love has turned life into a gnawing infliction. But the kids, unlike many contemporary lovers, remain incurable romantics, even in the face of bold rejection. Each Peanut, in spite of the fact that his love is unrequited, persistently pursues his heart's desire.

Lucy, too, is an expert in the art of one-sided love affairs. She attacks Schroeder with Valentine cards, devoted hours of listening to his music, and even open advances. The young genius, however, barely acknowledges her existence.

Schroeder's callous comment is horrifyingly typical of today's cool, career-minded, and self-interested bachelor, the man who refuses to be caught in a woman's mysterious web. Yet were his mind open to scrutiny, the faithful young lady would have a marvelous advantage.

92

HEY!

ZIP!

WHAT DO YOU THINK YOU'RE DOING?

NO FUTURE HUSBAND OF MINE IS GOING TO SIT AROUND HOLDING A BLANKET!

I'M NOT YOUR FUTURE HUSBAND GIVE ME THAT BLANKET!

NO!

Because mind-reading is not a successfully practiced art, the kids are forced to approach their loves in a straightforward manner. The Peanuts' tactics do not include fantastically complex plots calling for special parties, special commissaries, and special analytical thinking.

Although far from being equally crass, Sally and Lucy are very similar to the James Bond breed of woman—the woman who knows what she wants, stalks her man, but inevitably loses the prize. Schroeder and Linus, James Bonds in their own firm way, are good matches for these miniscule superwomen.

When it comes to love, poor Sally is a loser, like her brother. She reacts violently, but verbally, to the news that Linus has slipped from her clutches. Yet she broods on her loss without resorting to sleeping pills.

Even Snoopy, who can suppress most anything, gets all hung up over love. Like Sally, he resorts to a rather commonplace mollifier for his crushed heart.

According to Snoopy, his rejection was caused by parental pressure. "My girl friend's father won't let us get married," Snoopy says dejectedly. "He doesn't approve of me. He said he could never allow his daughter to marry an 'obedience school' dropout!"

Many young men today face overly concerned fathers and straight-laced mothers who believe nothing is good enough for their pink-cheeked darlings. And to think, Snoopy had such good intentions—intentions often quite different from those of today's males.

Snoopy would have been subject to much harsher criticism had he chosen a dachshund or sheep dog instead of a little girl beagle. He preferred to seek his mate inside the "beagle brigade." In our free-swinging society, young people very often seek mates their parents find unsuitable, inappropriate, and often impossible. The members of this revolutionary generation, however, do what they wish and not always what their religious or ethnic backgrounds would lead them to do.

After having made their rebellious selections, some of the ultramoderns even have marriage-ins in public parks and join hands on top of ski slopes. Today's hip generation has lost sight of churches, synagogues, and flowing white lace and orange blossoms.

The Peanuts, on the other hand, value the traditions of ideal love. In the search for a mate, they look to the stable elements of marriage, the unifying elements they see at home—love and respect. While many segments of today's society continue to sneer at such values, the kids still believe in the awe and the power one person exerts over another when in love.

Charlie is about as romantic as one can get. He loves i
a manner often applauded by fourteenth-century Frenc
troubadours.

He blushes, then turns pale at the sight of his belovec
He has confidants to whom he confesses his love.
He loses his appetite for almost everything.

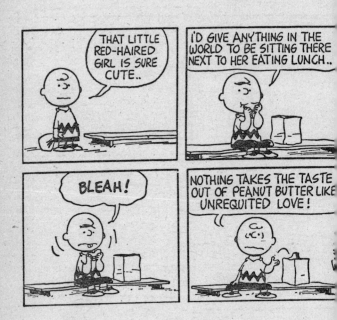

He worships the lady from afar and is afraid to a
proach her with a declaration of love.

He is in the clouds and unable to deal with the mu
dane and ordinary things of everyday life.

He composes poems about his lady and longs to gi
her tokens of his affection.

His demonstrations and protestations of love have th
fatalism of unrequited passion about them, indicating th
he couldn't really hope to have his passion returned.

These canons of courtly love were once discussed b
Friar Cappelanus, chaplain of Eleanor of Aquitaine durin

the Middle Ages. Today they are the required reading, rather than the practice of high-school and college students. In this age of frankness and free love, gallantry is a precept that lives only in the mind. Putting this precept into action is as archaic as the armor worn by King Arthur's knights.

Charlie Brown, however, is true to healthy, old-fashioned tradition. He loves his redhead from afar, hanging on to every indication that she is the woman of his dreams.

Lucy, in typical female fashion, shows her unfeeling by snatching the pencil from Charlie. And Charlie loses another chance to meet his red-haired little lady. But there is nothing Lucy can do about Charlie's romantic intentions. He continues to think about his "girl" and plots and plans another way to meet her.

100

The kids don't give up. They won't settle for communal living and loving. Sharing husbands and swapping wives is not for them. They're always in there fighting for the "one" they want.

Regardless of the pain, the Peanuts do not become disenchanted, moody, or bitter. It's tough going trying to pry Schroeder away from his piano or Charlie down from the pitching mound on the baseball diamond. But, you can never tell when someone will weaken.

7

•

BUT
IS IT ART?

A DISASSEMBLED CAR engine greets you at the museum entrance. Is it a work of art? The cacophony of mismatched musical notes. Is it art? The Peanuts kids, like most people today, are concerned with this age-old question of what art really is.

Among the little folks, however, a propensity for the traditional stands out. They prefer the classics: operas by Rossini; symphonies by Beethoven and Brahms; paintings by Thomas Eakins, Andrew Wyeth, and Van Gogh.

There isn't a member of the "beat" generation amon them. They tend to ignore the most pressing current fad They dress conservatively—hardly a long hair or min skirt can be seen. The kids are not even transistorized the compelling blare of electric guitars and autoharp Fads in music and art just do not exist for these tiny purists.

Look at Snoopy. He is the epitome of the art dabbl extraordinaire. Second to eating ice cream, music is o of Snoopy's favorite things. Most dogs are sharply a briskly whistled in to dinner. Not Snoopy!

Snoopy is in tune with the eminent classical composers. He has an ear for Mendelssohn, Brahms, and Chopin. Once, in a fit of musical ecstasy, Snoopy called a fellow Peanut "Papa Haydn." He literally stands up and flips for Beethoven.

Living in esthetic comfort and splendor is another of Snoopy's delights. His house has air conditioning, wall-to-all carpeting, a pool table and television set, a library, lver candlesticks, and a mural. One day a little rain fell to Snoopy's life (a leaky roof) almost destroying his ost precious possessions. Then the ever-present threat f robbery became a reality. Some acquisitive birds tried steal his prize Van Gogh. He sentenced them to hard bor. Finally, there was a fire.

But fortune favored Snoopy. His house was soon re-uilt, his Van Gogh replaced.

In his relish for acquiring art treasures and a tastefully decorated home, Snoopy has many human counterparts. But Snoopy is no copier; he doesn't get his "original" ideas from magazines. His good taste is not the result of buying the "right" books for his library or locking his silver candlesticks in a glass case. Snoopy's doghouse decor and cultural potpourri are strictly for his own pleasure and the pleasure of his infrequent guests.

While Snoopy enjoys most forms of art, Schroeder gets pleasure almost solely from music. Schroeder's world revolves around one art and one composer—Beethoven. A truly dedicated prodigy, he can almost always be found playing the works of this great German composer on his toy piano.

For Schoeder, exposure to music was love at first sight. He was introduced to the piano by that round-headed virtuoso, Charlie Brown.

Before long, he was playing the masters and composing original works. The first was "Rhapsody on a Theme by Schroeder." He was even given a contract by the "New York Philip Harmonic" to play at all performances before his bedtime, 6:00 P.M.

For Schroeder happiness is playing the piano because he really wants to. In that respect he differs greatly from many instrument-playing children of today. Schroeder is not tied to the piano by supermotivated parents who live vicariously through their children: "Make Mommy and Daddy proud of you"; "It's for your own good, darling"; "Someday you'll understand how important it is to have a talent that few other people have." Schroeder was spared these all-too-common pleas.

Also, unlike many of today's piano students, Schroeder is happy pursuing an antisocial occupation. He actually enjoys his life as a nonjoiner without any apparently harmful psychological side effects.

Schroeder's total love for music is reflected by his possessions, as well as by his self-inflicted persistence. He owns a music box that plays Bach in D Minor, a complete classical record collection, a bust of Beethoven on his piano, and a life-size portrait of his favorite composer for the bedroom.

Schroeder buys nothing simply for the sake of making a purchase or as part of some popular trend or fancy. What would Schroeder want with a Tiffany lamp in his music-dominated world? His piano is for playing; his music box and record collection are for listening, not for impressing his friends during dinner.

Although the other Peanuts kids are not as taken with any single art as Schroeder is with music, they all have knowledge and a nonaffected appreciation of the esthetic Lucy frankly admits that, little by little, Beethoven is winning her over. And, after hearing a Bach selection

112

played by Schroeder, of course, she unabashedly describes it as "beautiful." Lucy's knowledge of classical composers is considerable for one so young.

With their above-average knowledge and appreciation of the arts, the Peanuts kids might have a hard time understanding many of today's museum visitors. Succumbing to social pressure in order to be able to discuss a current exhibition would strike the kids as plain silly, a waste of time. They would wait on a three-block line to see a Rembrandt or Picasso if they wanted to, but certainly not just to have something to talk about.

Their knowledge and understanding of painting and music would also prevent them from making hasty value judgments. Even loudmouth Lucy might look with wonderment at the museumgoer who uninhibitedly voices his criticism from the center of the gallery hall, "They call that thing a work of art?"

Art criticism is one area about which the kids have little to say. Even though they lean to the classics and the traditional, they would be the first to admit that they really don't know what constitutes great art. Schroeder, the only artist in residence, goes as far as to say, "Great music is an ART!! Do you hear me?" he shouts at Lucy.

Lucy, in turn, once reminded Linus that "a true work of art takes at least one hour." And on another occasion in a fit of anger, she really got specific . . .

THAT CLOUD UP THERE LOOKS A LITTLE LIKE THE PROFILE OF THOMAS EAKINS, THE FAMOUS PAINTER AND SCULPTOR...

AND THAT GROUP OF CLOUDS OVER THERE GIVES ME THE IMPRESSION OF THE STONING OF STEPHEN...I CAN SEE THE APOSTLE PAUL STANDING THERE TO ONE SIDE...

UH HUH...THAT'S VERY GOOD... WHAT DO YOU SEE IN THE CLOUDS, CHARLIE BROWN?

WELL, I WAS GOING TO SAY I SAW A DUCKY AND A HORSIE, BUT I CHANGED MY MIND!

SCHULZ

In spite of their attempts to define art, the kids are anything but pseudointellectuals. In fact, they are remarkably "square." Surrounded by the more traditional art and artists, which they enjoy, they don't seem to be aware of the cultural phenomenon caused by the rock revolution. Talking to Schroeder, you would never know that teenagers are now controlling a mass medium—the phonograph record. Nor are they *au courant* about trends in painting and sculpture. To the kids, a collage is probably something you attend; a mobile, a gas.

Artists placing bodies on wet canvases and selling the imprints, painters hurling vegetables from a palette, cultural coffee cans and soft drink bottles reflecting the American way of life, geometric squares of colors painted in oil and labeled Composition II seem not to be part of their cultural interests. Pop and Op art, the current rages, just do not enter their minds.

The kids love the good things—music, art that is tried and true—good ol' Beethoven, Van Gogh, and Bach. They love meadows with green grass, songs with a melody, culture and the good life you appreciate for yourself.

8

·

A
NICE SHADE
OF GRAY

ALL THE PEANUTS are fast learning to fend for themselves in the business world. They are realistic about
success. The rules are pretty clear cut. You must say the
"right" things, things the people who count want to hear.
You must wear the "right" clothes—not flashy, just so they
blend in nicely and unobtrusively. And you must attend
just enough concerts, plays, and foreign films so that
you can be a hearty contributor to the luncheon conversation. In sum, you must create and uphold the going
corporate image. If you study your lessons well, you will
be able to take your place among today's successful
Xeroxed worldlings.

With the exception of Snoopy, the Peanuts are hard at
work applying these fundamentals in preparation for
their entrance into business life. The kids say what the
teacher wants to hear, dress appropriately for school, and
usually do what they are told. Even 'ol Charlie Brown,
the world's biggest blockhead, is aware of the rules that
lead one to success and prosperity—the American Dream.

Big business is a necessary evil that provides for many luxuries and extra joys in living. The important thing, and the kids know it, is to play the game the company way. Nonconformity, long hair, flip clothes, and be-ins have no place among business giants. With this knowledge, the kids are on the road to becoming smashing business tycoons.

The ability to attract others is an absolute necessity in the business world. The Peanuts regard this ability as a cardinal virtue.

One surefire way to become popular is to say things that will not enrage, inflame, or annoy other people— especially your business superiors. It is perfectly all right to promote harmless causes. But if you have strong feelings about religion, politics, or sex, forget them. In the business world you have to be *a*moral and *a*political.

The devoted corporate man cannot afford to offe[nd] anyone. For him, happiness is being a nice shade of gr[ay]. A certain amount of docility can be to your advanta[ge]. Being a "yes" man often pays off much better than ha[rd]-and-fast convictions or brash individuality. If you a[re] climbing the shaky rungs of today's business ladder, t[he] "no" man is someone to be admired from a distance.

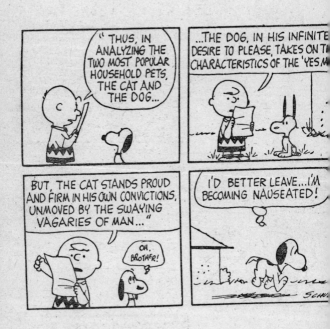

The most important aspect of ladder-climbing is [to] know what role to play—and how to play it. Timing a[nd] adaptability are essential: a smile for the superior w[ho] steals your best idea, then recommends you for a rai[se]. In spite of the fact that Snoopy lives solely for his o[wn] pleasure, he is an expert when it comes to adapting [a] proper façade.

123

Schroeder, although totally dedicated to Beethoven, realizes that it is sometimes necessary to assume another role, to play it the "company way." But role-playing is only a temporary thing with Schroeder. With a heavy sigh he would say that's how the game *has* to be played. Then it's right back to Beethoven. Schroeder is not about to sell himself and his ideals down any old corporate river. In part, yes! But completely, never!

Only Charlie Brown has trouble adapting to occupational situations—large and small. He is terribly afraid of being labeled a phony. And besides, as Psychiatrist Lucy points out, ol' Charlie gets some sort of neurotic pleasure out of failure.

If you are going to be a successful businessman, you have to win some of the time. And, in order to win, you have to fight a little. Or to put it in business terminology, haggle. Expert haggling is an art. Whether you are seeking money from Mom or a raise from the boss, haggling demands a certain amount of diligence and discretion. You cannot be too inflexible nor can you give up too soon.

Haggle for *your* price. A shrewd businessman never accepts the first offer. He works toward his price—and gives up only when he sees the back of a head walking away from his "business deal." Lucy's mom has the right idea, but Charlie still has some more lessons to learn.

A well-bred bargainer is rarely forgotten. He is usually the one closest to the office with new modern furniture and an overstuffed swivel chair (provided, of course, he obeys all the business commandments). Being successful is a hard road, as Linus so realistically points out. "Working one's way up" is hardly a primrose path of dalliance.

There are some instances in which the businessman can avoid haggling. In those cases personal contacts—whom you know at the top—will conceal your failings and slip you over the rougher business hurdles. More

often, however, even the most desirable personal con
tacts are not sufficient to sweep you uncompromised to
the top of the corporate ladder. Even Charlie Brown
world-famous manager, has to go beyond personal con
tacts in an effort to better his career.

In business and politics honesty and sincerity often
have a way of working against you. Linus obviously understands the subtleties that go into "good," effective advertising. His keen awareness certainly improved Charlie's
chances of receiving replies.

When it comes to big business and advertising, th
Peanuts are tough to fool. Madison Avenue is not abou
to "pull the wool" over their eyes. Snoopy isn't going t
let some irritating, downgrading commercial reappear o
his television screen—not if he can help it!

It could very well be that Madison Avenue needs more Charlie Browns and Snoopys to keep it on its toes. An openly controversial Frieda or two probably would not hurt today's advertising either. If Madison Avenue decides to make curly hair the vogue, Frieda will undoubtedly decide that straight hair is fashionable.

Linus also has his periods of mild revolt against advertising and business. Nevertheless, Linus continues to eat Snicker-Snack cereal for breakfast. Influence determines who eats what foods, who wears what clothes, who reads what magazines. Snoopy, who often protests the outrageous, is only too happy to accept the tangible fringe benefits of big business.

GOOD GRIEF! DON'T YOU HAVE ANY PATIENCE AT ALL?!!

THE SNICKER-SNACK CEREAL COMPANY SPENT FORTY-THOUSAND DOLLARS TO DEVELOP A BOX TOP THAT CAN BE OPENED EASILY, AND YOU RIP THE WHOLE TOP CLEAN OFF!!

MY HEART BLEEDS FOR THE SNICKER-SNACK COMPANY!

YOU'VE BEEN **REPRIEVED,** SNOOPY!

THIS IS **NATIONAL DOG WEEK**! THEY'D NEVER DARE TO TEAR DOWN YOUR HOUSE TO BUILD A FREEWAY DURING NATIONAL DOG WEEK!

YOU HAVE A SEVEN DAY REPRIEVE!

THANK YOU, MADISON AVENUE!

The kids are savvy to *all* the benefits of the business world. And like any hardworking businessman, they will take their profits whenever and wherever they can get them.

The Peanuts play the tycoon game and enjoy it. They are well aware of the musts and must nots of business. In the end, "you must be a joiner, not a fighter."

131

The computer is one aspect of our society, introduced and perpetuated by big business, that almost cannot be argued against. Although the kids enjoy disputing among themselves, they won't buck big business and its methods. It wouldn't be realistic. Who wants to reject our society as materialistic, militaristic, and capitalistic? Big business is here to stay! And the Peanuts know it and accept it.

9

·

THE FUN
IS IN THE PLAYING

WITH GAMES, according to Charlie Brown, "It's not the winning that counts, the fun is in the playing." Whether the Peanuts kids play football on a bed or run relays on a couch, they play for fun. The games they play are meant to be won. And if they don't win at first, they simply try harder. The result is a sports philosophy with a normal, healthy logic.

Part of this logic can be attributed to the openness and directness with which the kids approach each kind of game. When Charlie, for instance, finally wins a game of checkers from Lucy, the checker master herself, he is elated.

Of all the Peanuts kids, only Charlie and Snoopy let sonal motivation enter the game. They don't attempt ide their desires. Snoopy longs to cash in his sports els—usually juicy bones—to buy a bowling alley. Charlie yearns to have his athletic prowess disered.

Regardless of Charlie's and Snoopy's ulterior motives, y both enjoy the game. How many of today's adults— even kids under adult influence—still participate in rts for fun, for the simple spirit and enjoyment of the ne? Are our motives for pursuing sports as uncompli- ed as those of the Peanuts clan? It appears not.

Today's adult tends to bury the wholesome philosophy mplified by the Peanuts kids in what might be called rts manias, often with hidden motives. Each mania, in own way, is a reaction to society's increasing pressures.

137

Often, for example, sports become a way of life; they gi
meaning to life—something the Peanuts kids could nev
fathom. With too few opportunities to express individ
ality and ability, the fact that a male—or daring fema
—can successfully and repeatedly attack a sinister s
slope or ride a killer wave is extremely inviting. As
result, skiers, racing drivers, and super-surfers are today
heroes. Totally absorbed and dedicated, the sports fanat
is becoming more prevalent—whether he sails across tl
ocean in a *Tinkerbelle* or on a *Kon Tiki* or makes mod
cars and races them at frightening speeds. For the parti
ipants, each sport is a way of life, giving meaning to li
—a far cry from the Peanuts kids who sample a little t
of every kind of game.

Making games, or any single game, a way of life wou
demonstrate a loss of proportion to the little folks. Ju
look at Lucy. She forcefully admonishes Snoopy for spen
ing his day skillfully gliding across the ice.

The "sportsophiles," we must remember, unlike the
[Pe]anuts kids, are not just enjoying sports as side interests
[or] hobbies. Many of today's sportsmen find order and
[me]aning from something that was once just a hobby. The
[oc]casional ski bum has been replaced by thousands of
[wel]l-brought-up boys and girls who are finding their "an-
[swe]rs" in skiing the dangerous slopes. They follow the
[sn]ow to the tops of mountains and to the farthest northern
[poi]nts; some even count the days until winter restores
["me]aning" to their lives.

[ ]Not the Peanuts kids.

[ ]Linus was early exposed to the mad, mod sport of
[ski]ing. Sisyphus-like,* Linus labored diligently to build a
[ski] run. (Fortunately for us, the ones we use are already
[bu]ilt.) After several tedious trips to the top, skis dragging,
[Lin]us swiftly whizzes to the bottom.

[ ]And he didn't have to wait forty-five minutes in a tow
[lin]e and ride for twenty minutes to the top only to find
[him]self at the bottom eight minutes later.

[ ]Charlie Brown and his friends have innumerable no-
[tio]ns and occupations with which to add meaning to their
[liv]es—without getting bogged down in the single-minded
[pu]rsuit of one sport. They play checkers, they flip base-
[bal]l cards, spin marbles, fly kites, ride toboggans—always
[som]ething different.

[ ]Yet many adults today use sports almost exclusively as
[a m]eans of attaining social status and business success.
[ ]The candid Peanuts child would never understand brav-
[ing], a hot, crowded golf course to impress an important
[cli]ent. The adult who takes tennis lessons to get ahead,
[to]be "in," would absolutely startle the worldly Lucy. Only
[Ch]arlie Brown continually suffers from the need to be
[ac]cepted.

[ ]Who learns to play tennis or golf today because he likes
[the] sport? For the status sportsman, athletic proficiency
[put]s him on the "good side" of the client and shows the
[bo]ss what an all-round great guy he really is.

* A legendary Greek king condemned to roll a heavy stone up a
[ste]ep hill only to have it roll down again as it nears the top.

139

Charlie *might* understand the social sportsman's motivation. Yet Charlie really likes baseball. His pursuit of the game, even with minor neurotic undertones, is above all sincere.

Schroeder, like most of the other Peanuts kids, makes no pretext of his athletic ability. He merely plays for enjoyment or because the team needs him. During the game he has no qualms about talking socially to Charlie Brown, the boss of the baseball diamond.

Snoopy, too, is sincere in his enjoyment of the game as game. The Walter Mitty Dog doggedly punts a football including . . .

Today's social status sportsman often, but not alway.
achieves his "satisfaction" with little personal effort. Yo
can be sure his European-made skis will be scenically lo
cated in the corner of his apartment—very "in" indeed—
or near his office doorway on Fridays. And, if he has som
extra cash, the status man will own a boat on which
sip cocktails—after all, what else does one do with a cock
tail flag?

It is doubtful that today's status sportsman would b
open and frank enough to admit his questionable enthu
siasm for the game.

The man who pursues sports solely for its social im
plications is often the same man who finds it comfortin
to own the most up-to-date accoutrements for a goo
many sports—almost all of which he will never take th
time to try, let alone to perfect. How many bowling ball
ice skates, and ski racks sit brand-new, dust-ridden, fo
gotten, and discarded in dusty attics and basements!

The "equipment fanatic" purchases anything and every

ning to improve the game he is unlikely to practice play-
ng—everything from home pole-vaulting sets to the finest
and-carved African darts to the most expensive fishing
ackle. He enthusiastically discusses schussing and sla-
oming without moving from the toasty warm ski lodge
ar. His philosophy is clear: all you need is the gear to
imulate conversation and to experience "instant togeth-
rness." Not a bit like the Peanuts' simple philosophy of
laying the game for what it's worth, for fun.

For the Peanuts clan you own the gear only if you play
ne game—does one really need every conceivable acces-
ory? Snoopy has a skating hat and a football shoe for
unting. But he doesn't have stretch pants and a sleek
ur-lined parka to match. Snoopy just doesn't ski often
nough to own *all* the equipment.

For the well-rounded Peanuts cast, life is just too inter-
sting to go off the deep end in any particular area—even
ports, which are important to them. Occasionally, though,
Charlie Brown lets other motivations creep in.

THUS ENDETH THE
DIVING CAREER!

144

And he admits he's "a bit neurotic about sports." Remember how ol' Charlie flew his kite in the dead cold of winter, giving up only after the string froze. Then there was the famous Charlie versus the kite and tree duel. Life was at a standstill for eight days while Charlie stood holding the kite string, the kite being lodged in a nearby tree. "Now, look, tree! That's my kite you've got up there. And I want it back," he pleaded. A rainstorm finally brought him in—and the nation breathed again.

Snoopy's nobody's fool. If a sport's no fun, he backs away—on all fours. He tried a new game once.

Let the "sportsophiles" have their manias. Hobbies are hobbies; games are meant to be fun, the Peanuts kids would agree in unison. But many of today's befuddled beings have lost this simple wholesome attitude.

10

·

YOU
CAN BECOME
PRESIDENT

IF THE PEANUTS kids were old enough, they probably would give some serious thought to running as candidates in the next election. Their concern for politics is much more apparent than that of many contemporary grade-school and high-school children. In spite of the worldly and sophisticated attitude of today's students in contrast to the previous generation, most kids under voting age continue to prefer ball games and pop music to politics. The Peanuts, however, split their ballot: ball today, campaigning tomorrow.

149

Although these kids are politically minded, they are not partisan. They do not favor Republicans or Democrats, Conservatives or Liberals. Their only criticism is of people who are too busy to keep up with present political life or too busy to make their own commitment.

If the kids could have their way, they would commit themselves to all sorts of causes. They would probably join freedom marches and attend political rallies. One Peanut at least would become a Peace Corps worker. As a group the Peanuts would have made dedicated "New Frontiersmen." There is even the makings of a Mario Savio * in the crew.

* Mario Savio was the leader of the Free Speech Movement at the University of California.

Linus' tinge of dictatorship is not always confined to snowmen. During a school election speech, Linus paled the face of the principal with his wild-eyed ravings: "If I am elected school president, I will purge the kingdom. My administration will release us from our spiritual Babylon. My administration will bring down the false idols in high places."

Their zeal, however, is not always accompanied by total understanding of domestic or international issues. In this respect these youngsters and many of society's adults are rightfully similar. For example, the Peanuts have trouble explaining peace between nations even in basic general terms—and their difficulty is certainly understandable.

War, on the other hand, does not pose such inexplicable conflicts. The Peanuts may not comprehend the circumstances that lead to combat, but they would be the first to stand up and fight—no questions asked! If the kids had a war rule book, the anti-Vietnam-War supporter "Put down your arms" cry would be listed under the "don'ts"; "fight until you win" under the "dos."

As it does all kids, the subject of war fascinates the Peanuts. Linus has Thermopylean dreams of glory. His enthusiasm for war games is the antithesis of 1967's crusaders who wear anti-war buttons and preach "make love, not war."

The problems of national loyalty are quite lucid to the Peanuts. You fight when your country needs you; you obey the laws of those in command. It's as simple as that. The kids listen to Mom and Dad and the minister, so why not listen to the nation's leaders? To them, as to many children, the President of the United States is a wise

authority who always knows what to do. Every Peanut—
with the exception of Schroeder—dreams of being Presi—
dent one day.

As far as the Peanuts are concerned, there is only *on*—
chief in the nation. And they know that the chief must b
elected. But they also know that sometimes it takes a littl
maneuvering to get the man you vote for elected.

During a campaign strategy meeting Linus tells Luc
that he is going to pick Charlie Brown as his vice-preside
tial candidate. Lucy's first reaction is a caustic "Goo
grief!" Lucy reconsiders and finds the ol' blockhead ha
a "hidden" asset that might rack up a plus for their sid

Lucy accepts the fact that a "bleah" candidate may b
just what the voters unconsciously expect—and what th
President needs during his term in office. The candida
who stands for nothing offensive may be the decidi
factor for a voter who notes little difference in the par
platforms. All things considered, it might be a sage poli
cal move to have Charlie Brown on the ballot.

Strategic maneuvering is also important when a nomi-
ee must deal with mass media. The communications
industry is the candidate's link with the public. With mass
media on his side, always speaking of him and showing
him in his best light, the public grows to love the nominee.
And before they cast their votes, they recall his winning
smile, pleasing platform manner, or perfect tennis stroke.
The Peanuts would empathize with the candidate who
worries about his image. They would agree with the man
who solicits aid from a public-relations firm or advertising
agency. And if the candidate uses a makeup man to help
him present a youthful mien, all the better. The Peanuts
are realistic about their politics.

Although the kids do not as yet completely understand
the elective process, they certainly know all about shaping
an image. Charlie realizes that if the press is against you,
you as a candidate are in trouble. When Violet interviews
him for the school paper, instead of making his usual
faux pas, Charlie mouths the appropriate clichés.

155

The public draws on what it *thinks* it sees, hears, a[nd] reads. If James Reston of *The New York Times* and n[a]tional columnists Rowland Evans and Robert Novak [do] not think the "hopeful" is a good guy, he might very easi[ly] lose the election.

Television reporting is extremely influential too. It pu[ts] political candidates under worldwide scrutiny. A bad pr[o]file, a crooked grin can help to wash away a promisi[ng] political career. The Peanuts see and feel the power [of] mass communications every day.

157

Probably the worst thing that can happen to a prospective officeholder is being totally ignored. You simply cannot win even a relatively unimportant election if you a an unknown. In order to find out exactly where one stan with a voter, political candidates use polls. A poll w tell you precisely what you are doing right and what are need improvement. Linus is no political exception.

Nevertheless, Linus worries about the credibility of t results, particularly if the polls are conducted by an i partial pollster like Lucy Van Pelt. The "undecide segment of the school population disturbs Linus. "It's d pressing to think that somewhere in this school there a students who still can't decide to vote for a nice guy li me," he says.

DO YOU THINK CHARLIE BROWN REALLY COULD GET NOMINATED FOR PRESIDENT?

WHAT DO YOU MEAN, NOMINATED? DON'T YOU KNOW **ANYTHING**?

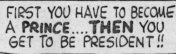

FIRST YOU HAVE TO BECOME A **PRINCE**....**THEN** YOU GET TO BE PRESIDENT!!

IT'S FRIGHTENING WHEN I REALIZE HOW LITTLE I REALLY KNOW ABOUT GOVERNMENTAL AFFAIRS!

Politics is not a business in which you can afford t
be second best. Contemporary politicians rely on polls t
keep them abreast of the image they are projecting. On
poll may tell the candidate that voters feel he is deficie
in knowledge of world affairs. Another poll may tell hi
that the majority of voters over thirty-five consider hi
ruthless. For the next few weeks that candidate can spen
his time brushing up on world affairs and finding jobs fc
people over thirty-five. The next poll will tell him ho
successful he was in bettering his popular image.

Although the Peanuts realize the power of a politic
image, and the importance of keeping in touch with po
ular opinion, they are almost unaware of the self-servin
reasons that motivate adults to seek public office. Publi
office and public service is a trust to them. As far as th
kids know, each elected officer regards this trust accorc
ing to the book: Elected officers are honest, law-abiding
loyal to their constituents, unselfish, dedicated, and, i
fact, walking Boy Scouts. Get elected to satisfy one's eg
one's thirst for power or unquenchable greed? Good grie